AUP
new
poets
9

Sarah Lawrence
harold coutts
Arielle Walker

Edited and with a foreword
by Anna Jackson

AUCKLAND
UNIVERSITY
PRESS

Contents

harold coutts
longing

Arielle Walker

river poems

Foreword

AUP New Poets 9 brings together three young poets whose work
has a freshness and vivid beauty, exploring longing, fragility,
romance and other tidal forces. Each selection is set within a
dazzlingly contemporary present, but each poet looks to the
past, too: 'People are the best time capsules', as Sarah Lawrence
puts it, writing with an awareness of the ways memory inflects
every instant; harold coutts looks back to John Milton who 'wrote
my gender as a poem that i memorised at birth', their own poetry
awash and aflame with personal and cultural history; Arielle
Walker finds points of resonance between Māori and Gaelic
pūrākau and traditions that offer flickering visions for the future.

Sarah Lawrence writes about conversations with friends and
encounters with strangers, dazzling coincidences and daily
routines, acorn-trading and breakfast-making, life as 'a series
of verbs', a process of growing up, growing hair out, growing into
relationships. These are poems full of life and full of all kinds
of *things*, including safety scissors, a carpet snake, a can of blue V,
pancakes, Lil Nas X, moan-rock, balconies, tobacco, a coaster, a
snake tattoo, budget margarine, maths problems, wily wildflowers
and a Morrissey poster, to list only a few. There is often a hurtling
quality to the poetry, with time moving rapidly from March to May
to August to October to December, as it does in 'Clockwatching';
with childhood, homes and places left behind, the poet in 'This
road' not knowing 'how to live with the fact that I'm leaving again';
poems beginning in mid-drama, sometimes in mid-conversation:
'"Actually, it's a Saturday", you said, but checked again' opens the
free-flowing abcedarian 'Weak nights'. The conversational quality
of the writing can look so much like artlessness that it might
take more than one reading to realise that the 'Love sonnets' are
written in perfectly metrical iambic pentameter, or that, with its
emotionally powerful rhymes and repetitions, 'Good people' is
an intricately constructed villanelle. There is as much attention

to form in less conventionally constructed poems too, with a playful and inventive use of line breaks, stanza forms, echoes, puns, spaces and absences, asterisks, ampersands and other forms of punctuation.

For all the lightness and lift of the poetry, it is not without depth or acerbity. In 'Something's melting; it's snowing again', the father, living in a hotel, is sent a chocolate cake for his birthday 'like the consolation prize for losing a game of family', a scene that could be straight out of a Raymond Carver story. The intensely felt present tense of poems like 'The edge of winter' and 'Everything', holding open moments 'stitching the crumbs / into an upside-down cake' or 'watching the freckles on your eyelids', takes much of its weight from the sense of the past and the future it also contains. And the vividness of the present tense is never felt so much as when it is captured in the past: in 'What I told the future', an old video is unearthed, on which 'I'm saying the same word over & over / & you can feel this throb of first / in the creaking camera / even then'. There is a fragility as well as a confidence in how time is inhabited; there is both nostalgia and optimism, grief and anxiety – and, deeper than anxiety, the brilliantly coined 'Pre-grief'. If people in her poems are time capsules of history, they are also full of explosive future potential to 'shatter into bloom', to 'renovate the five stages of grief', to leave each other, lose each other, find each other, see each other as magnificent, molten, fairy-lights lit, to be each other's lifeboat 'when the / walls are swimming'.

Fragility and exuberance can be found too in the poetry of harold coutts, whose selection powerfully conveys the rapture and anguish of romantic love. The romantic situations are contemporary, gender is understood as a cultural construct that can be deconstructed and reconstructed, but there is also a visceral force to these poems as they explore gender and romance in elemental terms. Death is as vivid a force as love, and imagery of gardens, tides, blood, mountains, soil and brine sits alongside the references to skinny jeans, mid-2000s phone charms, swivel chairs and Grindr hookups. Things in these poems can be found awash, asunder, betwixt, aplenty, aloft, sharpbright, ever-bleeding, pearled, splayed; they thrum, waltz, throb, gnash, lash, writhe, caress, chitter. There is little of the conversational about the sonnet 'i am growing a garden' which flaunts the brilliance of its rhymes – sequence, frequence, beacons and weakens; under, asunder, thunder and wonder; foundation and lunation; given and driven; flume and bloom, bloom, bloom.

Not only John Milton but Perseus and Andromeda, gods, souls and a Greek chorus are referenced in these poems which look back to the classics not for some kind of fixed or timeless beauty but with urgent questions and a passionate intensity. For all the intensity of the poetry, it is full of uncertainty, as full of questions as it is of exaggerated similes. The announcement of a kiss in 'i do not see you at all' is followed by the line, 'is that too homely? too intimate? too gay?' Gender is perhaps the most impossible mystery of all – 'can i sell my gender on trade me / can i use my gender to kill god / can i slow-cook my gender and feed it to my friends' are only some of the questions posed in the dazzling opening poem to the selection, 'my gender'. Over the course of the selection gender is both rejected and celebrated, exploded and reimagined; it is too much, intrusive, invasive, and at the same time an enigma, lacking, absent: 'my gender and lack thereof are arm wrestling on my ribcage' is the image offered in the poem 'i stole a line of this poem from someone else'. Well yes, these poems are funny – this is a selection that travels between the tragic and the comic and back again, leaving the reader both moved and dazzled.

Arielle Walker (Taranaki, Ngāruahine, Ngāpuhi, Pākehā) is a visual artist as well as a poet, whose work across the different media explores interconnections between land and language, migration and the ocean, roots and botanical resources. Her interest in form is apparent not only in the individual poems in this selection, with their beautifully assured layout on the page, but in the shapeliness of the selection as a whole. Opening with a form of *ars poetica* that is as much question as answer, the sequence moves in layers and circles, with the selkie figure of the second poem returned to in the penultimate poem, and the significance of this shape-shifting, yearning, elusive figure becoming increasingly resonant in relation to the developing themes of journeying and searching, ancestry and home-making, belonging and negotiating, story and memory, breath and skin. From the opening question – 'How can I write a poem that isn't first a body of water?' – the act of writing is related to the fluidity of the self and the inhabited landscape. This is poetry that is close to the lyrical essay in its concerns, as well as in the formal features like the headings, comparisons, italics, strikethroughs and footnotes that add so much to the poems, but without being centred on the lyrical 'I', more often speaking as we, or to you, giving instructions, sharing knowledge, questioning stories, looking to a shared future, bringing into it shared histories. The question 'ko wai au?' in 'the imagery of trees' follows – and is inseparable from – the question 'ko wai koe'. Observations are presented as invitations and posed as questions – 'see how they are as alike and not-alike as cousins?' the reader is asked in 'kānuka & mānuka' (from 'rongoā').

'Kānuka & mānuka' is the poem most clearly structured around doubling and pairing, with the verse split across the page, while the longer sequence 'rongoā' also includes alder and elder, heather and thistle, and lichens recognised as two symbiotic beings, algae and fungi, working together. The sequence brings together, too, the healing traditions of two different heritages, and brings into awareness the relation between plants and people, wholeness and absence, the riddled kawakawa leaves offering both a salve to the sting of lost words and a memory of colour to hold on the tongue. Words themselves are often doubled in these poems, in which things are salt-licked, battle-wounded, blood-sick, travel-feared, seaweed-caught, and in which we find fish bones, moon-pull, rivermouth, windsong, rainhum, salt lines, sealskins. The selkie of two of the poems is in itself a creature of two worlds, land and sea, and has many names – selkie, silkie, selchie, seal-maiden, finn-folk, maighdean-ròin, maighdean-mhara – without the stories ever giving her own name. Yet the doubling of the selkie's life is perhaps less important than the liminality, and the imagery of land and sea less emblematic than the image of the shore, 'the takutai moana, the shoormal / where sea meets sand.'

Reflections, repetitions, doublings and oppositions can be found
in all three of the selections in this anthology – the past and the
future, gender and the lack of gender, sea and sand, rivers and the
sea. But every binary opposition is open to confusion and creative
reconstruction, and participation is welcome: 'It takes a village
to raise the past', Sarah Lawrence writes, in a poem about the
questions bodies ask, while harold coutts's line 'i bide my time
and bite my thumb and bind my boredom to myself' reappears
later as 'i bide my thumb and bite my boredom and bind my time
to myself', before giving way to further unanswerable questions.
All three poets write of questions unanswered and questions
unasked, secrets ithheld and thoughts unspoken, times when, as
Arielle Walker writes 'we didn't have the / language' but all three
poets, too, demonstrate the possibilities that a depth-charged,
free-wheeling, formally attentive approach to writing can open up.

Anna Jackson

Sarah Lawrence

Clockwatching

What I told the future

People are the best time capsules.
Mum gets me monotone at the dinner table,
she gets me knotted like a womb-fresh foal.
I walk past that building sometimes & have
this full-body shudder of what it felt like to live there:
the smell of incense & Mary J, the
knock-knock-knock of faces
fish-eye through the peephole
in the door, but

people are the best time capsules.
Grace gets me pseudo-wise, leaking
cracker crumbs down her car seat.
Emily gets me fourteen again, flying
MH370 jokes that never land.
There's an ancient video on our old PC
from when I was still the only child.
I'm saying the same word over & over
& you can feel this throb of first
in the creaking camera
even then.
That awe that feels so special & isn't.

People are the best time capsules.
I wonder sometimes what I'll find fossilised
in your palm lines one day. What you've left in mine.
If it's toothache or budget
margarine or perhaps
another world altogether.

Something's melting;
it's snowing again

I'm sorry, it's seven-oh-two & I've kept you waiting,
don't shake your head, unbutton your eyebrows, I see you
shrinking in your jacket. did you know I was born late, born
in a snowstorm in cambridge ... & you were born too, what a
dazzling coincidence! if I've kept you waiting, that means
I've kept you, which, do you think that's sweet? no? well

you know, a state of being is a state of waiting ... but you
can enjoy the waiting if you'd like, or alternatively, you
can hate it & write poetry. do you think
one day you'll get married & fill the street with daisies,
or put some doves in a cage, or city pigeons you found on
the roof, & pretend love is not part of the waiting, too?

when my dad was living in a hotel, on his birthday we
sent him this big expensive chocolate cake, like the
consolation prize for losing a game of family. when something
is radioactive, it keeps poking tiny holes in people, until
one day all their hair falls out & they can't stand up,
so they have to roll to work & ask the barber for a comb-over &

there's this formula you can use to calculate when
radioactive matter is only thirty-seven percent of what it used to be
but, if you wanted, you could just tell me. is it worth the waiting?
if I could manage to believe in science AND sinatra
maybe i could become an astronaut. then I'd fly to the moon
without loving at all. yes, I'm sorry we're waiting. how do you
fill a graveyard with living things? it just seems so cruel.

Pre-grief

Dressing, in September, is just juggling
the elements. I'm always a bit mad at you.

Sometimes it's for how much you look like me. Sometimes
it's for how much you don't. Hiking, in this city, is just

looking at the same view from different angles, but I like
how the houses have to grow around the forest. They are our good warm squares,

our Jenga. An infestation. You kissed me once,
and I had to watch myself through your eyes for weeks. I hated you

for that, even though you had nothing
to do with it. Growing up is a process

of de-imagining. I watch the 3 p.m. bicycle exodus
from the footpath until I turn 13. I'm skating to the mall

with the kind of friend you don't realise until later
you are probably a bit in love with, and we are going to run away.

I don't ask her what it is she is running from. She doesn't ask me.
We steal a whole bagful of Maybelline, Ben & Jerry's, Lovisa earrings,

because those are the necessities,
then look at each other, choke, and never speak again.

Lost clocks / strange music

I live with three women and none of us have object permanence. We cut new
keys and bookend our days. Often we disappear and don't notice. Find bits
of ourselves scratching at the window when it's cold. Spend mornings in
the kitchen cracking eggs, cracking up, evenings blasting out our separate
speakers. Pissing off Katrina downstairs again. Making sound waves into
riptides: gangsta rap, girls who sound like honey, Lil Nas X, moan-rock. Like
we're fledglings and Saturdays are for flying practice. Lining up our eyes, our
pockets, our powders. Painting our skin space alien. Peter Panning for gold.
Turning fluorescent while we dance

and our bodies are painted time bombs. Telling each other in the morning
about things we're scared of. Flipping the iceberg. Flipping pancakes. Seeing
corners of our mothers in the way our mouths crease and sputter. It's the
same story: growing our hair out, but mostly growing

into each other. Watching the avocados sprout cataracts and the bananas
go brown. Wishing for terracotta, feeling ourselves black-and-white. Like a
silent film. Leaving rooms that dissolve behind us. Making lists of everyone
we know, packing them down. Making them fit. I'd like to look back on a year
and see it naked. See it as a series of verbs. Running up the wind. Thawing
on the couch. Saying *loser.* Saying *loser.* Saying *love you.*

Eden

It was me & you & grace, learning all about each other,
unzipping flower stems, inventing fire & music.
Before there was language there was talk, everything
sparkling with it: the set, the sun
stretched long & lolling,
the bluebells, the body I was learning
to use. Those were the voices we knew,
but once, a flower was a mother & she touched our shoulders –
she talked us to sleep –

& we dreamed of skyscraping, of another world
to turn on its hinges, to weave in & out
of. Is now our punishment?
Before there was language I saw it in you.
There is so much to say I am going blind.
I said, grace, are we flowers too?
Grace, are you pushing us up, up & out of here?

& grace was snake green. Grace had nothing to say.

The edge of winter

At the edge of winter, everything takes
on a heavy quality, as if May is sitting
atop the colour green & pushing it
into saturation. Stitching the crumbs
into an upside-down cake, I speak slowly
to strangers who blink like cats.
On the lunar eclipse I come home glitter-drenched
to a gaggle of gawkers on beanbags outside, late
for the hole in the sky.

(We all smile at each other.
We have forgotten our names.)

At the edge of winter, cold knits
itself around our skeletons. Cold is a second
flesh. Songs chase me across bars & time.
I pour my heart out on balconies & let
the words drip down & away with the smell
of tobacco, down through the alleyway by the record store
where we pore over the DVDs through the
window when the shop is closed, swear
we'll watch them all someday.

(We leave the stains of our fingerprints.
The mist of our breath.)

The edge of winter cuts a line down
my centre & from the gash I spill all manner
of things. I am philanthropic, even.
I ask a homeless man what he'd like
from the supermarket & he says a can of blue V.
One night we sneak into that place we used to live.
The air is cleaner & the walls are stripped.
I feel as if I have defeated something.
I turn pink then white
then pink again.

(In a different life, strangers are corridors I wander forever.
While I walk, I sing myself happy birthday, sure
I am being reborn, somewhere.)

This road

I don't even know how to live with the fact that I'm leaving again. In rows the
motorcars are water, white, blooming. It's comedy. This road is a production
line where I took my first steps; squint, see Chaplin grinning & spinning in
the spoke of a wheel. I walk slow, then fast. The cicadas whirr with the thrum
of machine. I am making something, piece by piece.

*

I am making something, piece by piece. I've decided I believe in astrology.
We are chatty & sweaty in the living room. We could all be visionaries &
not even know it. Last week, you said, 'I don't even know how to live with
the fact that no one desires me right now' & I've decided I believe in as many
things as possible. There are many facts we cannot live with.

*

We live without. We buy caged eggs. This road has the face of a stranger I
ripped from your dream; some nights I feel us healing, clicking & green; I
want to know everything about you. Charlie peeps through the blinds. On the
door of the campus toilet cubicle is a sign that reads: *maintain your belief in
love & humanity*. There is an unflushed shit in the basin.

*

There are many unflushed things. A cheap watch. Your cracked cell phone.
A carpet snake, once, that slithered through the pipes at my grandparents'
house & stayed, lodged, for quite some time. Flower petals. I am watching. I
am watching you unwind, unwind magic & shiny & plastic like a ballerina in
a music box; I pull them from my pocket. Headphones, tangled.

*

Headphones, unwound. It unwinds again. I listen how I listen when I am in between places; Adrienne, old friend, poured into the whispering kettle of an eardrum; this road snores & wakes. *There's a woman inside of me.* Listen; how it screeches. Screams? Scratches? Stretches.......& O! Steam! Steam all up through the cobblestones! All up through the sky......!

*

I don't even know how to live with the fact that I'm leaving again.

Good people

Good people die slowly. You'll die fast
In a freakshow headline, a clickbait tease.
That's something my body said. I didn't ask.

It takes a village to raise the past.
Cigarettes. The manmade beach. Grass knees.
Good love leaves footprints. Ours walked fast.

Mother made me take a street defence class
Where love put me in a chokehold, told me, 'breathe':
Love, a word my body said. I didn't ask.

In her casket, Mother wears a mask
Of bones that has her face & looks like me.
Good people die slowly. I'll die last

Of rope-burn. Tied to skeletons, tied so hard
I rattle every headline, shake to read
The words that bodies say. The questions bodies ask –

The body of our village & the past
Sprouts roots each year. Leaves. Cleaves the space between.
I'm scared I'll love you slowly. You'll die fast.
That's something my body said. I didn't ask.

Natural disasters

two years before, i sent emily flying
on the see-saw in ōtautahi elmwood park; screeching, i
sank into the tyre like a stone while
her kebab legs buckled up, up,
defied gravity for a single soaring second ...
when denim hit metal with a clap of thunder-thud.
she tried to laugh, then she cried,
hands clenched, showed the trees
the white-hot scar in the spiderwebs of her knuckles where
her brother once tried to cut her finger off with safety scissors;
i understood him then, trying to laugh, sirens
all the way to the gp, six-year-old skin quivering with the discovery that
people are not
paper

*

some lady opened a bookstore on the street by my house
which i thought was brave, like that time my mum told me
'we need two generations for this sort of thing'
when i bought three whole books the lady looked
at me very strangely
said, 'it's good to read the classics'

*

the day it happened, on the bus
to rutherford's den, emily was showing me how
she could fit her whole raincoat in her pocket when the
bomb went off (so it goes), and we hit the floor.
later, trying to laugh, emily showed me a new scar beneath her
eyebrow where her seat split her skin, the day
we didn't split the atom

*

in school we were the reigning queens of
acorn-trading, with bounty buried precious
in a sandpit grave. one morning, this kid stole all our acorns,
and tried to trade them, thinking we wouldn't
notice, but we did, and we didn't speak to that kid for
the rest of the year. another morning, the acorns
started sprouting, and we didn't know who to yell at

*

we were trying to be newsworthy, emily
holding a sign scrawled in crayon:
'don't be a fossil fool', really sticking it to The Man

later, we sat, foolish, legs crossed, shaking in the central
library while The Man shut 51 books

it was in the new york times

*

the month the streets were empty
my sister and i took a photograph in the
same shop window every night to see if we would change, somehow,
and we didn't, although some days i had toothpaste
on my shirt and once this big cargo truck drove past
and we swore at it, grinning

*

you'll see me in a fairy-light glow, talking into
a can on a very long string, stretched, in fact, across the cook strait;
emily is learning to fix people's bodies
and i am learning to read a lot
which she thinks is brave

*

ten years later, we embrace in elmwood park, slipping into the
snakeskins of ourselves, prodding away at the old
dreamscape, we try, we do, but we both know
there are chestnuts under the leaves, and
paradise ducks nesting in the riverbanks, and
i have a raincoat in my pocket

LIFE USED TO BE SO HARD

after 'Our House', Crosby, Stills, Nash & Young, *Déjà Vu*, 1970

Picture half a house, veins open & splayed out from the rafters. Two cats in the yard, like the song. Plums. Picture history, your imaginary friend, history that crashed its stone through this window when I was a whispered breath in the ache between two hands & before & before. Here is a civilisation you built. Here we teemed as maggots in the belly of a bird & here we snuggled in blanket nests to reality TV & here you thad to learn how to love me over & over & I have slammed every door in this house: this house which eavesdropped on every apology I have ever made & this house where we cried & cried & cried & cried. O you, you house of cards, O you, my home built on stolen land, O my cresting wave, there are things which were not perfect about you. First wallpaper. Then whole rooms. Now I take photographs of the stump of a cherry tree I once wrote a letter to, thinking it would answer. To renovate is a process of acceptance. Here is a civilisation you built. One morning we found the whole body of a previous house cat, crawled cold & shrinking through a vent & deep into the undergrowth to be dragged from the rubble at sunrise an age away, cracked & awkward, naked to the bone. Will you dance? Will you picture the honeysuckle creeping thick through the years & defeating every bad paint job that ever lived? This house is named Entry in a language you do not speak & to enter is what you have always done … into portaloos & the book of family passwords, into someone else's leftovers in the fridge, into whole new streets & outer space & space in the crook of my elbow, into Rome, into the frying pan, into places where you do not belong & then do. Today I turned a corner to tell you I'm reading that book you always talked about & you weren't there. Here is a civilisation you built. Here I will renovate the five stages of grief, find new things to deny & deny until I am ascetic & tin hat & screeching, tearing down the staircase like a mad wife while the world turns & turns & would you please picture me magnificent, molten-eyed with hair splayed out & wild, ripping every curtain from its rail & throwing matches high into the rafters to stick & bloom as it burns & burns & burns & burns & burns

Love sonnets

Cereal monogamist

you liked your toast with margarine & jam
I told you I remembered, & you smiled
I'd eat cornflakes, you'd show me 90s bands
that was my favourite hour there for a while.
last night I tried this maths problem in bed
& suddenly the math problem was love
if I keep taking calculus forever
I'll crack the answer. did you know that once
I found this cactus sitting on the street
then threw out all my wily wildflowers
thought, *this one I swear even I can keep*
you'd call it lovely, in my favourite hours
&   I'd make you tea with chocolate on the side
        I poured it wrong. the hardy plant still died.

Alone at the Kingsland Social

there is a pigeon flying at the glass
again, again, it hits the window pane
passersby blink & giggle, footpath mass
sing quick umbrella elegies in rain.   I know
I love you with that special paranoia
of being sure you've left something behind
in taxi cars, or kitchens, or street noises
or stretching raging oceans around rhyme.
I wonder what the bird sees in this room
perhaps a new dimension where to quit
is to want so hard you shatter into bloom ...
to try is to forget. love, I admit –
       I am the pigeon, typing in the dark
       but this you knew: clear café fishtank glass.

Morrissey by 'Morrissey'
(in five acts)

I.

This is the part of the poem I meet Sarah
tongue-tied & 15, trying to impress a boy in a trench coat.

O, it was magic, the golden age of tumblr & *Skins* UK, back when
the elevator scene in *500 Days of Summer*

still felt like a healthy legit way to find your soulmate.
Sarah thought she was deliciously special in her discovery of my genius.

As it turns out, I was simultaneously courting a whole demographic
of pre-therapy teenagers: the kind who hate themselves

in a 'GOD WHY can't I stop being so angsty hot esoteric & fascinating ALL THE TIME'
sort of way. She was disappointed when she found out – disappointed

but not surprised. She knows I'm a whore like that.

II.

This is the part of the poem I throw in a tenuous literary reference.
Something homoerotic. A scream. Perhaps 'This Charming Man' is playing
at New World

& you are tired of tongue-tied. He looks at you through the
gaps in the tomato cans & you look away. It is sad indeed that I am not just
a whore like that

but also a racist. It is sad indeed when you snap out of it & start actually
wanting things like happiness & real love. There are so many good songs you
can no longer sing.

III.

This is the part of the poem in which I am not enough.

When I was not enough, I became ironic. On her first day
in a new city, Sarah bought a horrifically ugly poster

from which I stared dead-eyed. Later that week, a new friend pulled
a chair to the wall & sharpied me with Post Malone's face tattoos. She spent

that year rattling with laughter, crackling with breath, chewing the black
from her fingernails & playing Hole with it stuck between her front teeth

IV.

The first time she peeled me from the wall was because of a global pandemic
but I still thought it was cruel. The second & third were because she was leaving

in different ways. The fourth time was because too much had happened
& she couldn't bear to look at me anymore

V.

This is the part of the poem in which I am a good party joke.
At 15 she was explosive & did not know it.

At 15 she had bubble gum in her hair & syrup in her bones.
She tries to remember my first name & it melts under her tongue.

I am not the poem. I am just the wrapping.
I like to think you would listen now.

Weak nights

'Actually, it's a Saturday', you said, but checked again,
Brushing lint from the wine cork. We'll stuff the bottle with
Candlewax & melt it with dinner parties; we are reusing, reducing,
Dragging up dregs of ourselves & watering them down.
Everything is a small word. I
Found bits of it pinging up the vacuum cleaner yesterday,
Got mad without wanting to, like who the fuck keeps leaving that shit
    out as if we
Have space for it, why do we own so many basil plants, as if I don't
    know what day it is, as
If I don't know all your middle names,
Jesus. We'll grow violent cooped up like this, like those
Killer whales in the documentary, with legs grazing under the table.
    Wiser me would tell you:
Life is a collection of gaps between showers –
Maps, ridgelines, longitudinal distances – &
Nothing is there, too. But only if you're listening. When we inevitably
    run out of cash, then
Out on the streets won't be too much colder. Heating's expensive.
    So is trying. We save for a
Party to spend it kissing someone in a corner
Quietly, thinking this would be so much easier if we were on the internet,
    when
Really, if I behaved how I do on the internet, I would be sociopathic;
    I would say,
'Same', when I see you on fire, & leave the room. Silent
Television dinners will, sadly, have to do for now. I have spent too many days
Underwater & too many nights stuck between
Versions of my own face, until I see yours, like a lifeboat when the
Walls are swimming, ask for
Examples & I'll pretend I'm not an alien, pretend I didn't come here
    because of you,
You & parts of you, just like always, us in our final forms, you in laughter
    when I'm all
Zonked out & dripping down the kitchen sink.

Dear Karenin,

after 'Dear Orlando' by essa may ranipiri

I am writing to you from another language, as people, somehow, always are. I hear it scattered amongst the 5 a.m. birdsong at the train station; it's hearing someone breathing, quietly, amongst all the satire. Karenin, you come from a world in which even a dog is thinking, but in mine, only I am thinking, and I remember you most of all because you were lonely. I, too, am just trying to do the right thing, reading the right books, loving the right Gods, growing as small as I can, letting the years fossilise my heart into a stone to skip across the great lake . . . it's that sinking feeling, and fast sometimes. Is that silly? I am writing to you, Karenin, because I saw someone dressed as you. I see him everywhere. He is my father, crying in the hallway. See, you'll wake up one morning and you will be in love, and it will feel so important, like missing a faceless ghost, so you'll search, and search, until you turn away and realise you were missing the person you almost became. It's cruel aestheticism, like watching a crowd at high school graduation, all thinking they will change the world. And you will change the world. You will change the world by changing the world as little as possible. Look at all the grass, growing green and green for miles. Can you see it where you are? I think that you are every man I know, crying for all of the forgiving, all of the fathers loving and shrinking, loving and shrinking. I do wonder if it is the same. You can pick up all of the ripples on the great lake, trap them in a jar, leave them fizzing in her handbag, like bright spring words you picked and left to die. You can. For now, there is a little speckled sparrow, silent on my windowsill, and I thought of you.

Everything

begins & ends with
nothing –

a place I feel far from at Willis Street New World
with its endless rows of beans, breads, yoghurts
in different brands. You're here & I hate you

for trapping me on your slow clock, here
where I can't stand still without someone glaring
to get past me with a trolley, or
wheelchair, or

small creepy child. I have never been angry

like this, not in stonefruit season
when the bay is warm, the sky wrung out & stretched
by the clothespeg hill pines, when
the sun arrives early & stays late like

a bad party guest, but
then again, I have never been
a four-legged organism like

this, watching
the freckles on your eyelids & the shape
of your teeth while you just hold me

up like a mirror, you,
kettle on, waiting while
I try to tell you everything & sometimes
do. I hate you

in a very unglamorous way, mostly
because you know me & wish I was better

as if I haven't done it too: wished
I could unzip my skin & crawl out

of me

& we've both done it, tried
to contort these awkward bodies
into something bigger than themselves
beneath the hard bellies of men & that

is how we learned to love. How boring, how
fruitless, the rhythm

of my ancestry. In the window
across our street, a man is
bench-pressing a coffee table. I see flashes

as of a grand plan: a coaster, an armpit, a snake
tattoo. Below him the paint
of his door chips –

unzips a little, the first sliver of nothing
as it reasserts itself – nothing:

a sore & temporary
loser. It always wins.

Clockwatching

I'm a Siamese twin in a tin
box on scaffold street, finding my rituals, finding my
cucumbers, half-eaten, rotting in the fridge. It's March and my lies are young
cities or phones ringing in my pockets. I think about you then, sucking

the marrow from my scoliosis spine, making me empty for filling. I
walk through a ghost and it's you before I blinked you off the waterline
of the waterfront. When the moon had a heartbeat and slid down the sky
you asked it for walls without cinderblock

and days without pain: you, a ghost before I knew you
were a shark, as scared of me as I was. It's May. I'm dealing you
lies at a ribbed picnic table. We choose our favourites, rig the game,
unreliable narrators of our own double lives. Or August

and I walk like I'm covered in small mouths, all swallowing
the rain. All gulping down jungle juice
and blood orange gin, gulping and sputtering on
the sidewalk / no, it's October and I'm lying here with everything we wanted.
Look

how small I am under crisp cream ceilings, living the same
anaesthetic day with you hooked on my fishing line, watching me through
the water of a paddling pool, or dreaming in an uber
where I wake up to you screaming and you are

the wind. It's December. I'm turning 20 in three days. I'm turning to
you lying next to me, lying to me, passed out in the ket net at the same time
I'm being born, branches stacked above me like veins,
looking at you from the echo of your own paper face. If I laid out every vein

in my body I would be long enough to stretch around the Earth. Instead
I'm mopping you up at closing. You scratch at the automatic door. It's been
five years and I walk through a ghost again. The bus home is late
and you're right, I was lying. It was all true.

We go into lockdown again during my second ever shift at Sal's Pizza

This is how the world ends.
Not with a bang (or, actually, a whimper)

but with the Spotify playlist 'This is Jack Johnson'.
That's the only thing they play at Sal's Newtown. On loop. Forever.

When Melvin gets The Call it's a real postmodern moment. Poor Melvin.
He's stuck understaffed with the trainee for the most traumatically busy night
of the year

because apparently all people want to do in the apocalypse
is buy $40 New-York-style pizzas.

This is how the world ends. Melvin is whizzing, making buffalo wings
& cheese sticks & pep wheels & combos with stupid names.

In this moment Melvin is God & I
am the main character of a rags-to-riches film

about a clueless country bumpkin who moves to the big city to become a star
while working on the side as a ridiculously incapable waitress, except

I am her before the montage set to a Blink-182 song in which
she learns how to actually be a waitress & comes out three minutes later

gliding effortlessly around the restaurant while the chef looks on in begrudging pride.
Which is a longwinded way of saying that I am shit. I fuck up three UberEats orders

& have a secret panic attack to 'Banana Pancakes' in the bathroom.
It's a real postmodern moment.

This is how the world ends.
At home my flatmate is making TikToks

about waiting for me to come back with free pizza.
Instead I stumble off the bus like a zombie, decidedly pizza-less, so

we spark up in the kitchen & use our last eggs to make supermarket brownie mix,
get that shiver of change all over. When I text my friend what happened,

he replies, *that's a real postmodern moment*
to which I say, *not the right word bro.*

Today we took the bikes to the hills

& it was good to feel close,
yes, good, even if you talked

over me sometimes & wind
caught us hard the whole
way home & you lost me on
the downhill & yelled into
the receiver that it was all my
fault & it was good, yes, to
hear you laugh at my clumsy
& flinch flustered when we
ordered the same meal in
the same voice, even if i
chose salmon & you chose
mushrooms & i saw then
our fingers crinkle in all
of the same places. at the
top of the peninsula you
showed me the carcass of a
military base where they
manned a cannon in WWII to
keep the bad guys out &
isn't it funny how they waited
for five years in uniforms
& no one ever came & after that
we both thought of the same thing
& you said you could've quit
sooner if you'd really wanted to.
i had to look at the ground for a
while. you looked at the water.
on the way back i saw four
bikers who looked like you
& the sunset spread tender
like a bruise & there was this man
in a hang-glider screaming at the

sky to put him down &
when i made it to the harbour i
called you from a four square

where we spoke in the same voice & yes,
it was good to feel close.

Hide & seek

This morning I cracked the shell before you told me
you ran out of gas & the egg lolled on the fry pan
in a stagnant pool. We glared all hungry. There are things

you can't take back. You are growing a sunflower on
your patio & now it is taller than both of us
but we are still growing too. I said I was scared, mostly

that you would grow tired of me &
you said I was always making things too complicated.
If you could write our tombstone it would read:

sometimes we were happy & sometimes we weren't.
Remember before I knew you how we used to go walking just to brush hands
& stutter & make freckles & we were walking once

when I was halted dead by the elastic band of
the reflection of the clouds in a gutter puddle
& I stood teetering like a bowling pin daring you to

say something & you did. That night you wrote a song to
the rattling of my shoulder blades as I opened my eyes to the world &
cried   *come find me, come find me, come find me, come –*

Real-life origami (to unfold)

Oh my girls look so pretty there
at the vegetable market, cardigans
& kūmara stuffed into green hemp
bags. We are a tangle of knees
dressed like actors in a festival film.
We are beginning to look like each other.
It is nice to be the youngest people
here, warmed by the body heat
of cool thirty-year-olds who pay their
power bills. The city is beginning
to pepper with faces I know. I can't
leave our house without seeing at least one
man in a fisherman hat. I can't leave our
house without saying at least one hello. Yes,
open your orange before we are home, it
is nice to squeeze stories from the rind.
Yes, I am here now & I am no longer
quite anonymous. The city is beginning.
I have never felt so brave.

Hopscotch

The foam-chequered tyre. The cupboard-stuck throng.
The breath of the sky. The yesterday song.
The trip of the leak. The nail-crack scream.
The stitch of the cup. The coconut cream.
The gingernut snap. The throat-hiker hitch.
The bait-knotted back. The cotton-mouth kiss.
The huddle for warm. The papercut hip.
The smoke alarm lack. The Ritalin drip.
The everyone saw. The swing of the mourn.
The playground is empty. You pick up the place.
The pieces of tide reassembling. You portrait you triage you freeze.
The sudden unthinkable ending –

harold
coutts

longing

my gender

my gender is a prince guitar solo
my gender is the shrill HA joanna newsom makes in 'colleen'
my gender is karen o screaming 'stress' over and over again at the end of the
yeah yeah yeahs' 'mysteries'

i bide my time and bite my thumb and bind my boredom to myself
in the depths i ask questions:
can i sell my gender on trade me
can i use my gender to kill god
can i slow-cook my gender and feed it to my friends
i get no answers

with my gender i have a card house comfort
with my gender i am cavernous
with my gender i learn to curdle in the funhouse mirror

john milton wrote my gender as a poem that i memorised at birth
having been read it every day by a caring parent
and then i attend university to be taught it by fellow poets
eyes burned out at 9 a.m. from behind the podium
while i doodle my freedom on the refill

i bide my thumb and bite my boredom and bind my time to myself
foolishly, i'm asking more questions:
can i leave my gender with a grindr hook-up
can i reupholster my gender into a swivel chair
can i enchant my gender to make it more powerful against undead creatures
i know i won't get answers

with my gender i am a beast of flux
with my gender i am a mediocre poet at best
with my gender i am caught in the headlight

i'd much rather read any other poem by john milton
which isn't saying a lot because i quite like *paradise lost* and i fucking loathe

my gender
consider me always just slipping out the door
gone for a quiet moment or returning to bed –
eden's fruit contently stuck between my teeth

worship

if i open my mouth will you fill it
head tilted as a pitcher
am i terracotta from 2200 BC
waiting all this time
for ___*

affront the sunlight
knelt for hours in waiting
now held in tune
canvassing silk with lurid tongue
all's awash with honey
given by bumblebees
curtailing the queen's own supply
for unfamiliar lust
have they sculpted in drift
to form a new husk?
coagulation in daylight
as two merge endlessly
hold me, lover eternal

here for the moment
to coalesce these rivers
into a world of worship
beneath this heaving form
i see god in the half-light
i hold faith in the seconds
of urgency
baptised in the afters
again and again

---
* him, you, them, anyone

i haven't driven a car in six years

the dead celebrities
are living under my dermis
leasing their homes from
the poets whose work i've read,
underlined, and then forgotten about
between all of us
we still can't drive a car

getting behind a steering wheel
is an evacuation of function
mice streaming out of my pores
to nest elsewhere
the garage won't be as warm
as the crust of my core
or as nourishing

the car begins too pertinently
and i am handed the power of death
at a wrist flick and inhale
the swerve of movement has no favourites,
in that it has greed eternal
only stopped by physic's limitations
and the panic bloom within me

from the bed of my blood
comes the collision
tear me apart for the media coverage
trickles of torn metal like snowfall
or dandruff on a pillow
now rest at your feet
it will taste metallic

vindictive

where is god when you hate him most
cowardly changing face to hide
always leaving before – you cannot finesse omnipotence
is he hidden in your shadow
so when you swing confrontation
he moves with you as the sun sees fit
does he tiptoe past your fuming form
a quiet creeping of nonchalance
as you curse him like a flog on flesh
he is on the precipice of present
but not quite listening
aeons of anger would lull one to sleep eventually

they say there's a man in the sky
i ask where?
and they point as if i asked for directions
above us is a cloud that looks like a bitten apple
next to the blaring sun, cold and uncaring
again i ask where?
they point behind me and the dance begins anew

pubelessness

welcome to the reclamation of my hair birthright
the bush is a crown resting at the breath of my penis
the permanent wave of my private time
puberty's valley beseeches me
naturally bejewelled and tender

for years *they* want my moonlight skin scraped
slaughter-ready for *their* raptures
prostrate and aerodynamic
tongues roll cartoon-like on the floor
crushed in the dance of my smoothness

a greek chorus clung above my thighs
reprimanding in the bathroom lowlights
in heed i banished pubelessness
now cherishing the bloom it invites
returning slow like birds to roost

it's like this

if gender is a taste i am cutting out my tongue
big scissors for the drama
i will oil & sharpen & kiss them goodnight
the cutting day is marked on my calendar
i throw a party, for which i bake
my friends cheer as i slice

      & bleed

if gender is a dream i am sleepless
how many coffees can i drink before my brain explodes
like a confetti cannon, or pop rocks on my cut-out tongue
i sell my bed because i am beyond it
leaving smiley face feedback on trade me
think of the books i can store in the space

      & behold

if gender is a promise i am oathless
breaking words like bitter tchotchkes
smashed ceramic on the floor of whoever's query
a prelude to bloody footprints
clotting the carpet for extra crunch
making my landlord's veins boil

      & burst

if gender is something people assume about you based on appearances

      & stereotypes

well, i guess that's unfortunate

i do not see you at all

i am drinking about this heat
your backyard sweats with us, three against the afternoon
this summer of lust has me bewildered by your touch (a reprise)
leaving imprints from our leg hair communion
kiss me or else i could die, my lover

i am thinking about how you got my face & the curtain behind
the sweat on your upper lip is an oasis happily bathed in
i mewl under the width of your thumb
lost in the power held against me
cut an ocean in half & coddle me

i am building you out of this hangover
eyes closed against the soft of your bathroom
the slushied memories drifting back like cement
a yearning foundation to delight by
i crawl back to the you i have created

i am waking you with a kiss, a joining & greeting
is that too homely? too intimate? too gay?
it is enough to look at you, no clothes & exhaustion
under the lamplight i close my eyes like so
i do not see you at all

hi and welcome to 'i'm tired' with harold coutts

i am without my bones
mould me into carpet and lay me down
thus i might get some rest
i saw the sunset and now it rises
mocking the mountains of my eyelids
as i lurch home

twelve-hour overnight shifts throw you down a cliff
then snap your ankles after helping you to your feet
there's no fault in thoroughness
the sweat gluing my clothes to this shell could grow an elm
i will cut off its branches to make splints
so i can make my way to bed

pulling the covers over my head one thousand times
only for the sun to wink full and constant
it unravels and i am threadbare
what offerings can i make to stop the sun
i would collect the blood of every soul in a pitcher
and tip it in the maw of whatever for one hour's peace

i am growing a garden

stems of lavender burst through skin to be cleft; a sequence
to be observed. dark shades against a cream, a peach – under
dragon-fruit lips. 'twixt mine own kissing approach, asunder
they become. vampire smile draws me in with frequence.
your cheeks simmer as roses – petals below as beacons
through the dermis – crackling round as cutaneous thunder.
irises from home behind filaments of pure wonder,
a blink and eyebrow arch so careful and yet it weakens.

i am growing a garden and you are my foundation
in the sense that i am sowing the seeds you have given
me. the water washes over me, given by the flume
to be conditioned for your return at next lunation.
i cannot wait for the touch, the unfurl, to be driven;
i cannot wait to catch your vision and to bloom, bloom, bloom

**there isn't a manual on when you're writing someone
a love poem and they break up with you**

i woke up to type words
about the singing and snoozing waves
to be edited, to be changed
from waves to wind to
anything

i dreamed about your shoulders
the muscles dripping down into your arms
or maybe they'd be crafted there
a structure

i spent a day letting the words
in no way final simmer and flicker

now what do i do

i stole a line of this poem from someone else

oh my lord, i am playing with knives
i'm starving but i'm not together
i cannot collect my ligaments enough
to sway to the kitchen

my gender is inside my room,
and my lack of gender is tar in my arm hair
gluing my body to itself,
but now my gender is picking up my favourite sweater and walking out of the
room without saying goodbye
and my lack of gender unlocked my phone and is remaking my tinder

i shot sharks in an arcade
and sunk four balls in a row
but nothing is enough without you, dear

(imagine me coiled on a hard surface,
glass of wine in hand
i am wearing only red
i say this to you with complete calm
now imagine the opposite)

my gender and lack thereof are arm wrestling on my ribcage
their elbows pushing against my new tattoo
kneading it under my bones
'til i am $100 cooler on the inside
i forget what they are fighting about

i'm beginning to forget how to be in love
but i can't forget the safety

the ex-boyfriend is back in town

i can't stop thinking about the shape of your fucking arm
i'd roll over in the mornings and it would be the edge of the horizon
an albatross soaring above
golden frame in a museum where gods dress down so they can attend in peace
aphrodite herself stops, peruses, readjusts her handbag, moves on
i've built a house out of the space before

i will have a son just to watch him die, gag at his scent over fire
and his sight on a silver platter at the table of zeus
so the king of gods will wrath me into wolf-shape
kin with lycaon of arcadia, fool of all fools
because i am falling through the air forever at the thought of you saying, 'hello'

i want to run down the waterfront growing hair and claws
a jaw jutting out from my face with gnarly yellow fangs
eyes the colour of poppies or cartoon blood
and howl at the moon, my mother
so that if you see me on the street you won't recognise me
so that if i look into the waters of te whanganui-a-tara i won't recognise myself

and so the museum stands in tatters, glass is floor confetti
sirens thrum like synth from the songs i'd hear when you'd hold my hand
and i am sitting, howling at the moon of your arm
the only piece intact

i had sex with the man who broke my heart a year after the fact

i have held this skin for days;
would you say it's molten?
gods' lips have blown hot air through your pores
and caught a soul alight

what if i became the yellow of my lamp's glow
held myself to and slipped under
i want to want to curl in you
nestled at warmth and centered

we shift over the mattress
leaden and slick
our mouths wishing fitness

the room collapses with us
contagion tearing drywall
coating us a new shape

in parting there is veracity
separate dressings / separate goodbyes

the door clicks finality
it's not easy to wish you back from the dark

cooking eggs for one

i waltz under street lamps
my shoes' slick resplendence
carries over the divide
i am kept in time

above is the blue that hugs in starlight
i'm praying to any god bored enough to listen
that i can waltz through the night
they shuffle their cards and consider

in the morning i cook eggs to placate the hearth of me
there's a place for your shoes, still
i have missed you enough to fill all the walls i exist between
but never enough to call you

the alcohol continues holding me down
roped into the spotlight of my sheets
seeping under my skin
and i am displayed just so

for i am a loner in the waltz
prophesied in the motions of habit
as a god plays a joker, winning the round
and it was i who shuffled and drew

my hometown has its talons in me again

reluctantly welcoming my dishevelment into the circuitry
of sunrise sonbigot sunset
like rows of teeth gnashing a dense meat
overcooked to the point of arduousness
i am spat back to the plate and scraped across
a hopeful for the compost

my form is detrimental
encouraging the rats and vermin nearer and nearer
with pings and blips on screen they announce arrivals
clawing through the compost bin to find me splayed
can they sink their teeth / lash their tongues /
can they fuck the husk and writhe a time

left for decomposition comes the quiet
pulsating as the talons drill further
birthing a fear of movement and exploration
so i am stagnant in the mild vegetation
stripped forever by the rats of pieces once important
to forget them all together

i long to be turned over
mulch intermittently exposed to daylight's fingertips
feed me eventual to plants aplenty
lacing the garden with my consciousness scattered
a stage where i splay my arms at the presented crescendo
for an urged reinvention of my most based cells

this too will kill me

i yearn with my whole ribcage
splintering my cellophane chest
in blood crinkle communication
never aloft & incognito
all to know about me is bleeding out
splattering under each footstep

can i grow a partner from the greenery
bloodfood offerings over mulch & soil
sees the landscape sprouting who i need
gnarled & arresting they court me
if i want to be held i am crushed
sun bleaches bone & branch all the same

or burn me at the stake in a meadow
wildflowers the only witness
for one trembling kiss
the last taste before consummation
is the pressed lip
then this inferno marriage engulfs me

i could greet the ocean with a keening
my pleura won't hold oxygen kindly
this great expanse of blue needs the room
i covet the brine as it fills me
drowned by the worth of all my weight
so i can be caressed lovingly forever

tee double u

i spend a lot of time thinking about swords
       knives too, any blade will do
       gift me a bouquet of dirks
       maybe an abundance will wipe the slate of my brain
       i will mount them on my walls & polish them sharpbright
       i will kiss/hug/love/wear them as accessories
       stabbed through my calf in a critique on fashion
       i'll hang mid-2000s phone charms from the hilt
       to clatter with each step from my ever-bleeding leg
           (would the scab crust over continuous & crunchy
           or flake forever in competition with hansel & gretel)
       fuck a skinny jean, i have no need for a suit pant
       i'll buy knee-length skirts & dresses to hoist over my head
       so as not to knock & enrage this open wound of beauty

i spend a lot of time thinking about
(it feels so obvious to say)   death

       not the weeks of dying or decomposition
       but the second it occurs & finalises
           (does the last rasp of air ache the lungs
           is the soul hurried or slinking away)
       i imagine the grim reaper beckoning with one impossible finger
       snagging souls like dust in shadows making leave
       sorting threads for hells to claim them
       fraying edges struck as if by lightning
       i have seen a dying & a corpse & tried it all on for size
       quietus always chittering behind my ear
       harmonious whispers of carrion & hearse processions
       how can i escape death when it's all life asks of me?

in the afters

do you experience love in cascades
little showers of pure feeling
they speak so much but say so little
love is a ramble // love is a curse
all to be lost as the tide goes out

listening to 'peace frog' by the doors in his car on the peninsula
i am struck by fragility
the stars are watching his first touch
and they twinkle at my continuation
a deadlock of passion as we overcome ourselves

the consumption of sex rocks the car
vibrations flow to the bedrock
each a message to hell of the fun we're having
the windows fog for our secrecy
as we jut and rut in the front seat

in the afters we dress
he promises to keep in touch but i know
we are drawn by the fragile tide
lust is a scramble // lust is a first
the feel of his flesh lingers

bad brain

i wake up in the dirt i'm in the dirt it's under my nails it's in my pores there's dirt clogging my tear ducts and sitting on my tongue bad brain says get up you fuck get up you're in the dirt which is true i am in the dirt bad brain says move your arse there's dirt in your tear ducts how did you get it in there i say i don't know the dirt moves from my tongue to between my teeth the taste it is bitter and sad but there's too much dirt i can't cleanse my mouth maybe the taste of the dirt will become my new religion i will pray to the taste of the dirt by holding it in my mouth forever bad brain says you're so useless i can't believe you got dirt in your tear ducts i try to cry but there's too much dirt so my eyes ache and the skin around them swells as the tears collect like diamonds buried deep i try to get up so i can wipe my eyes but there's dirt all over my hands as well and the rest of my body too pushing and holding me down bad brain says get up with so many exclamation marks i could turn them into a shovel if there wasn't so much dirt i try to lift my arms to grab them but the dirt is pressed so warm around me bad brain yells you fuck you lazy fuck get up get up but the dirt won't budge so i can't budge i wish the dirt would fill my ears so i can't hear bad brain anymore so i nuzzle into the dirt i let it fill me

i let it cascade across my crushed body and then i hear bad brain no more

a response to 'perseus and andromeda in landscape, from the imperial villa at boscotrecase'

she is pearled, a prize
i have lost my eyes, for what else is worth my sight?
the wind kisses a storm across her
nibbles leave her polished still –
maybe a bite would do
arm splayed & taut, the other rested
power of blood absent under chains

perseus, the magpie in this occurrence
erect at desire; at andromeda
he is near swallowed in a fog of green
(a swamp of landscape & seascape
each becoming the business of the other –
both without asking)
with lyre & cloak he is stuck in advance

the cache guarded by one with slobbered chops
crested as a beacon to things that susurrate in the night
coiled in assumed waters
tail peaked with faux-torpidity –
o, ketos, to devour such & live is impossible
emergence into death is a fate awaiting;
farewell.

the limitations of my body are throttling me

i want to be cut careful into twenty pieces
& fed to sharks purely because i think they're beautiful
i want to scream, 'why am i so sad all the time' from a mountain top
only to have god call down, 'check your birth-chart, dipshit'
i want to play the harp at my own funeral
so i suppose i'll have to suck off a necromancer & get some lessons

imagine a new life coiled inside me
suckled to my nutrients
a symbiotic growth i will cherish in the dusks & dawns
i feel the kick & twist as it sleeps
i feel its heartbeat & humming 'twixt my singing
i feel it grow & we are dancing accumulative

on a tide it comes, & i hold my child
i hold my child & it is all i know
have you ever looked at a fantasy & become obsolete to the world?
i have seen my motherhood & cried at its distance
i am touring this desire in all moments, visa clutched tight
said goodbye to my loved ones at the airport & never looked back

it's not that i hate my penis it's just that i wish it were detachable
i would transmutate my body in the bathroom mirror
& the earth's spin is concurrent still
on a whim i could reattach
& either way i am whole
in this world my scars return to the bedrock

i am but a haunted house without the luxury of terror
cemented in closure & a lack of landscape
in the half-light i wish i was glowing to fruition
but the leds are phasing out the harder i plead
bring me a jackhammer & a high-vis vest
would you come force my hand?

the sharks in the wine-dark sea haven't surfaced
jaws open for my pieces
lay my purple on the mountain top in rudeness
so god knows i don't care what they have to say
i twist the phone-cord around fingers in eager desperation
waiting for a call that won't alleviate at all

loose doxycycline at the bottom of my tote

rattling against the taut fabric
like little mistakes
reminding me of the flaws i cherish
expelled from the loose-lidded container
by a crumbling eventuality

my doctor
swabbing the back of my throat
as i politely avert my gaze
like a dog on a chewed-up couch
waiting for my mess to be cleaned

deftly i pick lint from the surface of the pill
it is still a little dusty
but diligently i swallow it as prescribed
the pharmacist said i can't lie down for two hours after taking one
i time my rigidness

i've learned to avoid eyesight
as the nurse pierces my skin
the needle feels like a harpoon
as it withdraws my wine-red blood
i hope my choices don't betray me this time

could

could she be half a hill burnt
still alight with the promise of spreading
lithe & waiting for the wind's tutelage

    the fire steals the last beer from your fridge
    & before you can say *what the fuck dude garage project isn't cheap*
    it's whirling down the hill

honey touched & hapless
she is the hill 100 years post-burning
lushly sprouted in recuperation

the ocean claims & she walks right in
waves kissing her, loving tender
& she dives below for joy

    & the water takes out the recycling
    the can crushed post-drink & compacted in plastic bag
    without choice, it waits

she is the greeting of rushed fire & complacent water
steamed eagerness emits
& she was all she could

poems about boys

my first order of business in this poem
is to discuss how i want to stop writing
      poems about boys:
it felt aimless and painful to be entered the last
my asshole is no odeum for a performance
churned forth from loneliness
      dancing among the boys again and
abiding disregard from the masses is
a hurtling of bones; ceremonial over parapets
falling is an art form if you wink on the way down.
      my eyelid is working overtime

i'm going to throw up my arms and say,
'what's the point?' to my reflection for four hours;
      the last time a boy made me feel anything
was when i listened to 'sophie' by goodshirt
a week ago. pressed replay on the footpath
and the wind grabbed my hand
      a more romantic act than forced flowers
can't believe togetherness comes from alcohol
and still learned loneliness. kissing in the moonlight
because we miss the touch. now i want to
      scour my skin of you

my second order of business in this poem
is to actually discuss how i want to stop writing
      poems about boys:
i am immortalising those who wrong me
and those who i have wronged. it holds a sourness
to my lips and parts them like a gate
      sucking dick only does so much for the psyche
but my, have i flown. until i find a love that stains
my skin, stubborn around each arm hair, i will stop.
the moon will hawk a name at my feet
      and then i will write again

Arielle
Walker

river
poems

a poem is a fluid thing all wrapped up in fish skin

How can I write a poem that isn't first a body of water?

How can I write a poem unless its surface is formed
from the borrowed skins of seals and salt and seaweed
and its blood runs in the swell and roll of waves and
moon-pull of tides and its bones are pieced together
from the calcified skeletons of a million
                              tiny
                              fish?

I cannot write a poem in a drought

How can I write a poem unless it rolls (a ready-made
river) out of the side of a mountain and runs gleefully
forward in a rush of eddying currents towards the sea
        so that all I have to do is hold out a hand to unravel
                the slightest fraying edge of its fluidity, and
                        spin a new yarn from its depths?

How can I write a poem unless I *become* a body of water?

How can I write a poem when I am still
piecing together the currents that form me still
tracing back along the saltlines that pool in my veins still
searching
     for the point
          at which my rivers
              merge
              into
           the sea?

I cannot write a poem until the rain returns
and raises the tides and floods the riverbanks and all
those fragments of fish bone and sealskin are pulled
back together into one whole
body of
     water

here are all the ways the story is the same

The story always begins at the takutai moana, the shoormal
where sea meets sand[1]

The story always reminds us that there are
rocks
on the shore[2]
where they first meet

(The story always skims across the how and why of their meeting,
notes that he stumbles upon her by 'chance'[3])

The story always includes
     a sealskin
     a sea-dress
     a cloak
     a cap or
     a kākahu
     a covering which means that

the story always tells us that she is uncovered
on discovery

---

1 It is always nighttime, it is always moonlit, it is always
    just   dark   enough

2 The rocks are where things can be hidden – people
    and shed skins
    and secrets

3 The intent, it's implied, comes later, so we can't assign fault

The story always gives her kind as selkie silkie selchie seal-maiden
finn-folk maighdean-róin maighdean-mhara[4]

The story always lingers on how
álainn ātaahua beautiful bonnie bòidheach lovely
she is

The story always centres on an entrapment, a betrayal[5]

The story always reminds us that there are
children[6] she will leave behind[7]

The story always ends
with her returning to the sea.

---

4 But never her name

5 Sometimes the betrayal is at the beginning
   in the stealing of sealskin, sometimes near the end
   with the trickery and trap of cooked kai
   but it is the same betrayal every time:
   he   stops   her returning to her kin

6 The story forgets to remind us that children are made
   of earth and salt water
   and belong to both-worlds and neither-world
   always caught inbetween

7 The story forgets to remind us that sometimes
   she takes them with her
   The story forgets to remind us that
   this is her choice to make

the imagery of trees

after Jenny Bol Jun Lee Morgan

we slip under many branches
sink
beneath their weight

falling away means the (ngā) ties or binds (here)
are broken. the base of the tree is usually unseen
the base (pū) of the tree (rākau) is too huge to hold

yesterday was mores and lores
tomorrow we could reimagine, *may not emerge immediately,*
is this belonging?
negotiating a methodological landscape beneath a kākahu
of saturated sky, stand firm. *Stories will take root*
and spread – our tūpuna knew this, i tuku iho, i tuku iho

we know it bone deep, ~~no invented imaginings or mere talk but~~ bloodmemoryandsong,
(aspects of which are difficult to 'measure', held in layers not lines)
these are *the base*
　　　(pū) of the tree
　　　　　(rākau)

if we should cause offence hold it close, ehara nāu, ehara nāu

we are but children after all and we slip
beneath
the
weight

never mind, *roots draw the water. ko wai koe, ko wai au?*
should we add another branch to the rākau?
write culture into the text, italicise and strikethrough the myth
of it, rewrite it, carry it, hold it close

fall into it? *a rendition of the imagery of trees*

rongoā

harakeke

karakia to Papatūānuku, to Ranginui, to all tūpuna
give thanks for their gifts
'ngā taonga whakarere iho'

never take the mother or father or child of the plant
trim the edges of the blade and cut away the keel
return the remains to the whenua
make a small slice in the flesh of the leaf
strip back the skin until the fibre is laid bare
take care of this plant body
as if it were your own body
miro the muka against your own skin

steep the remnants in river water
and they will give you the first soft light of the rising sun.

heather & thistle

go to Scotland as summer is tilting towards autumn
the braes will be kiver'd in lilac
              (the heart of the thistle holds the same shade, but the
                                thorns get in the way)

fold the sprigs into a bed, lie to sleep and dream of home
(the one that holds your heart and the other your bones)

travel the paths around Taranaki, heather is
a weed here – still, take only what you need and no more
don't linger on the missing and the lost, move on

the new shoots will simmer green to gowd
                            (the thistle leaves no imprint at all)

yarrow

to journey safely: search among the rolling hills of Éirinn / find the
flowers of the athair thalún growing amongst the seamróg / pull off ten
leaves and throw one away / put the nine others in a white cotton cloth
and tie with a string around your neck / do not pass an elder tree / take
the flowers and simmer them / half into a sunshine yellow / half into a
healing tea
      drink deep

kānuka & mānuka

kānuka stands tall   mānuka has thin skin
with leaves that don't scratch   that flakes and peels
or bite or sting (a soft touch)   (and a barbed tongue)
tiny flowers   it holds its branches small and close
and scented leather bark   and its seeds closer

see   how   they   are   as   alike   and   not-alike   as   cousins?
a   consistent   case   of   mistaken   identity

but they are both healers
honeystarters
firemakers
colourfixers
sheltergivers
teatrees

they   prepare   dry   earth   for   new   growth
they   prepare   fibre   for   new   colour
they   lead   the   way   so   that   when   we   later   follow
the   paths   made   by   their   roots
there   is   already   something   to   come   home   to

alder & elder

never ever cut down an alder tree   (instead)
stroke the catkins, watch the wood bleed fearnóg to ruam
let them soothe your weary feet, there's still so far to go

take only the leaves for green,
        the twigs for red,
        the fallen bark for brown

never ever cut down an elder tree   (instead)
stand under the branches on Samhain and watch
the *daoine sídhe* ride by
let them lift the weight from your chest
let them teach you how to breathe again

take only the fallen,
        the shed,
        the ripest fruit
steep the bark into dye and the berries into wine

docken & iron

go straight to the roots, they hold all the power
they've grown down deep; dig in deeper
tear them from the earth
forget that they're manuhiri too
hack at them until you have only slivers left
let them stand in for your own whakamā
soak them for days, boil them for hours
add iron pulled from slick dark bog mud

you're aiming for the deepest black, but every time
nothing will come out
but grey, grey, grey

angiangi / feusag a' ghobhair

lichens are born from reciprocity

> *(stumble across this knowledge, learn in awe that lichens are
> not plants, learn how they are not one individual but two
> symbiotic beings, algae and fungi entwined together, how
> their relationship could have been a parasitic imbalance of
> power with one draining the life from the other but instead
> they learned to give, learn how each provides what the other
> cannot create alone)*

they are the ancient ones, they built the foundation for us all to
grow upon

kawakawa

look first for the leaves with the most holes
(the hearts should be riddled with them, it means they are
healthy, it means that others have already eaten their fill
and left you with only the strongest pieces)

meld the oils into a salve
to soothe the sting of lost words
sliding from your stumbling tongue

the crushed leaves will dye a shade of soft olive green
that fades as fast as summer does
(better to drink it in and hold
the memory of colour instead)

whatu

karakia to Ranginui, to Papatūānuku,
to Hine-te-iwaiwa, to all tūpuna
give thanks for their gifts
'ngā taonga whakarere iho'

form the whenu from the whenua that holds
your heart and your bones
the whakamā and the mamae
and the joy, too

make the aho from all you have gathered here
harakeke and heather, kānuka and alder,
mānuka and elder
thistle bite and docken soothe
simmered kawakawa and yarrow
the colours that reveal their roots
and yours, too

lay your weaving at the salt-licked ocean edge
let the waves swell and pull it from you, a joining, a gift in return
and (to bind it, and make it whole) they will give you
the last soft light of the setting sun.

dream futures from a plant placed beneath your tongue

Yarrow, bloodwort, athair thalún, sanguinary, seven-year's love,
devil's nettle, thousand-eye: a healing plant for the battle-
wounded, blood-sick, travel-feared, lonely and lost.
Cut into stalks or held against the eye, placed
beneath your pillow or your tongue,
it can divine futures.

In one future we have woken Rūaumoko and the air
is hung heavy with ash and haze, we were warned not to rest
in the shadow of the maunga, our tūpuna are not ours to own
but we did not listen – and so the maunga have wrenched
themselves from their resting places again to
settle old scores and we are all caught
between viscous molten lava
and andesite
In one future we
have coated Papatūānuku in
a thick concrete skin and all our memory of green
is passed down through whispered stories, all is not lost
if we are willing to look beneath the surface
but instead

we keep building out and up (we know Rangi and Papa are
longing to be closer but not like this, not held
at the points of skyscrapers)
In one future, Tangaroa has risen
far beyond the shoormal, the takutai moana, far beyond the sleeping
shifting tides. The islandfish have slipped their nets, and some of us
now live beneath the waves, sealskinned, shifters
while others are
seaweed-caught and
salt-drowned
In one future Tāne-Mahuta walks
the ngahere, which stretches once again from coast to coast, and we are
gone but the world is not silent, not silent at all with the calls of birds
and slow slide of lizards across stone and windsong and rainhum and
the rushing
and roaring of the
tide

In one future we remembered to look back, and to listen,
and things are good, and things are whole, and things are tika,
but that future flickers and is hard to see clearly through the
dreamhaze

trust with your skin

after Lehua M. Taitano

It will tell you when the stones get too sharp, the sole bruised, and
sense the biting before it succumbs to poison, a warning.

It slips you whole into the mudsoft flood path, moulded, held in slick
grey clay weight upon your tongue: you have inhaled the earth now,
a reversal. With your skin the watershock comes twice as fast: the
tides   pull,   pull,   pull   that   way
a warning too   *you are ready are ready are here.*

Your skin was made all surface, open. Something to peel away,
whole,   can   you   sense   it?   The   shifting.
The ochre saltwashes stone to sea, paints you in its path, the earth
has claimed your surface. The water, waiting.

before the sea, the bones

sheep

we went searching for bones and found
a row of them, five, bright white against the black sand

when we dug deeper the line
curved beneath the surface: seven bones, then nine

we found the feet a moment later and so the
whole took shape beneath us, unseen, we mirrored it

we stepped back
we didn't have the
language to give them rest

bird

further along the rivermouth we found another bone
alone, this one, slender but bright

folded beneath were feather remnants
and the sinew still clung, firm

i knelt down, asked
too fast *could it be mine for the taking*
carved the bone from its place
and left

at night i wake to bird calls

a flock of them, midnight heavy and haunting
a singing sigh for a missing piece
a seeking, a return

river

i follow the river sinew back along the salt-sweet
spine
to the mouth
retrace our footsteps
alone, this one, in the morning bright

sea

light: kneel down, return the bone
to the sand, feather buried

the sea sieves the sand from my feet
softens the line back, surface smoothed

and i return to you, then we
keep searching
for bones

skin

she crossed the ocean, held buoyant by the surface swell
shed her skin in each new land she came to
folded it neatly
into a locked chest
(or had it taken from her)

without her skin she could not go back to the sea

she left her words in the old land
tucked away the sruthán, the sionainn, the tír-dhá-ghlas
into hills and riverbeds

she grew accustomed to her new form
learned to exchange salt for soil, built instead
upon another's ocean of grass, her brine beginnings
passed on through memory
and then myth

she crossed the moana, motu to motu
i tīhore ia i tōna kahu kekeno
and stepped onto the shore
her kākahu kept close for safekeeping

she grew accustomed to her new form
held in an embrace between maunga and moana
she put down roots

until she was stolen away, and stolen again
and her words began to shift
kupu crushed like gravel
into new consonants
the takutai moana, the paringa, the tai
and her kākahu
taken from her

without her skin she could not go back to the sea

she crossed the haaf, shaped by the waves
shed her skin upon the draa
an folded it neatly
into a locked kist

without her skin she could not go back to the sea

she grew accustomed to her new form
learned to exchange salt for soil, built instead
upon the body of a mountain
her brine beginnings buried in the earth

she locked her words away too
dialect smoothed like seaglass
into new vowel shapes
the shoormal, the skröf, the lönabrak
forgotten

but see, here is where her stories come together into one
for though they all shift in the how-where-why of it

in every telling I've ever heard

every time
every time
every time

                                        remember?

the story always ends
with her returning to the sea

all rivers
after Airini Beautrais

all rivers meet the sea.

rain collapses the silt and soil, we made here home
dug in too deep and caused rifts, fall in, *e toto ana i te whenua*
we have sliced the tīr, *it answers to your blood and bone*
caught in the brackish tang of tides

drift the currents, salt to sweet and back again
set them to root in the mountains
there's still more to come, we stopped listening
to our tūpuna *the wavelength*
never alters it's just harder to hear

the problem is the sky never stopped missing her
they'll pull close again *the wind concurs*
we'll all meet the sea eventually. *Like water does.*
to gather: Huihui, all rivers.

Notes

Clockwatching

'Something's melting; it's snowing again', 'Pre-grief', 'Natural disasters', 'Love sonnets' and 'Weak nights' were all first published in *Starling*.

'LIFE USED TO BE SO HARD' first appeared in *The Spinoff*.

'Hide & seek' first appeared in *A Fine Line: New Zealand Poetry Society Magazine*.

longing

'my gender' was first published in *Out Here: An Anthology of Takatāpui and LGBTQIA+ Writers from Aotearoa*, Auckland University Press, 2021.

'it's like this' was first published in *Stasis Journal*.

'i am growing a garden' and 'i stole a line of this poem from someone else' were first published in *Starling*.

'there isn't a manual ...' was first published in *Poetry New Zealand Yearbook 2018*, Massey University Press, 2018.

'poems about boys' has been previously published in *Starling, Best New Zealand Poems 2019* and *Out Here: An Anthology of Takatāpui and LGBTQIA+ Writers from Aotearoa*, Auckland University Press, 2021.

river poems

A version of 'a poem is a fluid thing all wrapped up in fish skin' was first published in *Stasis Journal*.

'here are all the ways the story is the same' was first published in *Sweet Mammalian*.

'the imagery of trees' and 'trust with your skin' were first published in *Turbine | Kapohau*.

Parts of the 'rongoā' fragments were included in the lyric essay 'untangling the aho', written for *Tupuranga Journal* with the support and guidance of essa may ranapiri, as was an earlier version of 'dream futures from a plant placed beneath your tongue'.

Other versions of 'dream futures from a plant placed beneath your tongue' were published in *Oscen: Myths* and *No Other Place to Stand: An Anthology of Climate Change Poetry from Aotearoa New Zealand*, Auckland University Press, 2022.

'skin' was first published in *Oscen: Myths*.

'all rivers' was first published in *Tupuranga Journal*. Pieces of this poem draw from Airini Beautrais' collection *Flow: Whanganui River Poems*, Victoria University Press, 2017.

The title of 'trust with your skin' comes from the poem 'Bare your back to outside air. To sun if it's a Sunday. Recline with a friend or stand-in. Trust with your skin. Loose ten lines for transcription. Across your spine, scapulae, your dorsal rib pinch, tender', in *Inside Me An Island* by Lehua M. Taitano, WordTech Editions, 2018.

Pieces of 'the imagery of trees' draw from Jenny Lee Morgan's paper 'Māori Cultural Regeneration: Pūrākau as Pedagogy', which was presented as part of the symposium 'Indigenous (Māori) Pedagogies: Towards Community and Cultural Regeneration' with Te Kawehau Hoskins and Wiremu Doherty, Centre for Research on Lifelong Learning International Conference, Stirling, Scotland, 24 June, 2005.

Sarah Lawrence (she/her) is a Pōneke-based poet, performer, musician and pizza waitress. She recently dropped out of law school to study acting at Toi Whakaari: New Zealand Drama School. Her parents are thrilled. She won the Story Inc Prize for Poetry in 2021, and you can find her writing in *Starling*, *Landfall*, *A Fine Line* and *The Spinoff*.

harold coutts is a poet and writer based in Te Whanganui-a-Tara. They have a hoard of unread books and love to play Dungeons & Dragons. Their work can be found across various New Zealand literary journals such as *bad apple*, *Starling*, *Ōrongohau | Best New Zealand Poems*, *Poetry New Zealand Yearbook*, and in *Out Here: An Anthology of Takatāpui and LGBTQIA+ Writers from Aotearoa* edited by Chris Tse and Emma Barnes (Auckland University Press, 2021).

Arielle Walker (Taranaki, Ngāruahine, Ngāpuhi, Pākehā) is a Tāmaki Makaurau-based artist, writer and maker. Her practice seeks pathways towards reciprocal belonging through tactile storytelling and ancestral narratives, weaving in the spaces between. Her work can be found in *Stasis Journal*, *Turbine | Kapohau*, *Tupuranga Journal*, *Oscen: Myths* and *No Other Place to Stand: An Anthology of Climate Change Poetry from Aotearoa New Zealand* (Auckland University Press, 2022).

First published 2023
Auckland University Press
University of Auckland
Private Bag 92019
Auckland 1142
New Zealand
www.aucklanduniversitypress.co.nz

ISBN 978 1 86940 988 3

Published with the assistance of Creative New Zealand

ARTS COUNCIL OF NEW ZEALAND TOI AOTEAROA

A catalogue record for this book is available from the National Library
of New Zealand

Design by Greg Simpson
This book was printed on FSC® certified paper
Printed in Singapore by Markono Print Media Pte Ltd